SUSAN B. ANTHONY

ON A WOMAN'S RIGHT TO VOTE

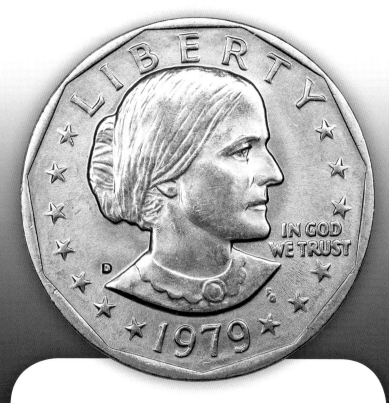

REBECCA SJONGER

CRABTREE
PUBLISHING COMPANY
WWW.CRABTREEBOOKS.COM

CRABTREE
PUBLISHING COMPANY
WWW.CRABTREEBOOKS.COM

Author:
Rebecca Sjonger

Series research and development:
Janine Deschenes and Ellen Rodger

Editorial director:
Kathy Middleton

Editor:
Ellen Rodger

Proofreader:
Wendy Scavuzzo

Graphic design:
Katherine Berti

Image research:
Rebecca Sjonger and Katherine Berti

Print and production coordinator:
Katherine Berti

Images:
Alamy Stock Photo: Pictorial Press Ltd: p. 16–17
Library of Congress: p. 6 (top center), 37 (center right)
  Bain News Service, publisher: p. 40
  Brady-Handy photograph collection, Prints
    and Photographs Division: p. 38 (right)
  Harris & Ewing, photographer: p. 6–7, 37 (bottom)
  J.M. Lathrop & Co.: p. 11 (botton left)
  Manuscript Division, Susan B. Anthony
    Papers: p. 3, 10 (background), 24–25
  Ohio Historical Society, Columbus, OH:
    p. 34
  Wust, Thomas, artist: p. 9 (right)
  www.loc.gov, Susan B. Anthony Papers
    Collection: Screen Shot 2018-11-14 at
    2.13.37 PM: p. 12 (inset)
National Archives and Records Administration,
  Identifier: 306684, Petitions and Memorials,
  1813–1968; Records of the U.S. House of
  Representatives, 1789–2006; Record Group
  233: p. 27
Ohio History Connection (MSS0116 Box 54):
  p. 35 (bottom right)
Shutterstock
  Jose L Vilchez: p. 12–13 (background)
  JStone: p. 43
  LEE SNIDER PHOTO IMAGES: p. 5
U.S. District Court for the Northern District of
  New York: p. 9 (left)
Wikimedia Commons
  Andrews, E. Benjamin. History of the United
    States, volume V. Charles Scribner's Sons,
    New York. 1912: p. 29 (bottom)
  Association (White House Collection),
    John Vanderlyn: p. 29 (top)
  Daniel Penfield: p. 42

Encyclopædia Britannica, Library of Congress,
  McRae?: p. 35 (bottom left)
Engraved by G.E. Perine & Co., NY: front cover
Harris & Ewing: p. 33 (bottom right)
Johnston, Frances Benjamin, 1864–1952,
  photographer: p. 38 (left)
Library of Congress: p. 8 (right)
  Bain News Service, publisher: p 11
    (center right), 41 (bottom left)
  Brady-Handy Photograph Collection:
    p. 8 (left)
  Thure de Thulstrup (1848–1930),
    restoration by Adam Cuerden: p. 20–21
LSE Library: p. 30
Mary Garrity Restored by Adam Cuerden:
  p. 33 (bottom left)
M. P. Price: p. 26
NARA, Clerk of the House: p. 41 (bottom left)
National Archives of the United States:
  p. 19 (left)
National Association Opposed to Woman
  Suffrage: p. 36
National Portrait Gallery, Smithsonian
  Institution, Randall Studio: p. 35 (top right)
Outlook 6.25.1919, International Film
  Service: p. 41 (top right)
Souvenir History of Niagara County,
  New York, 1902, page 56: p. 22 (bottom)
Tagishsimon: p. 22 (top)
The Revolution, edited by Elizabeth Cady
  Stanton, published by Susan B. Anthony:
  p. 23
U.S. National Archives and Records
  Administration: p. 11 (bottom right), 18
W.A. Rogers, Harper's Weekly: p. 33 (top right)
All other images by Shutterstock

Library and Archives Canada Cataloguing in Publication

Sjonger, Rebecca, author
    Susan B. Anthony : on a woman's right to vote /
Rebecca Sjonger.

(Deconstructing powerful speeches)
Includes bibliographical references and index.
Issued in print and electronic formats.
ISBN 978-0-7787-5240-0 (hardcover).--
ISBN 978-0-7787-5255-4 (softcover).--
ISBN 978-1-4271-2184-4 (HTML)

    1. Anthony, Susan B. (Susan Brownell), 1820-1906--Juvenile
literature. 2. Speeches, addresses, etc., American--Women authors--
Juvenile literature. 3. Women's rights--United States--History--Juvenile
literature. 4. Feminists--United States--Biography--Juvenile literature.
5. Suffragists--United States--Biography--Juvenile literature. 6. Women
social reformers--United States--Biography--Juvenile literature.
I. Title.

HQ1413.A55S56 2019   j324.6'23092   C2018-905569-3
                                                   C2018-905570-7

Library of Congress Cataloging-in-Publication Data

Names: Sjonger, Rebecca, author.
Title: Susan B. Anthony : on a woman's right to vote / Rebecca
  Sjonger.
Description: New York, New York : Crabtree Publishing Company,
  [2019] | Series: Deconstructing powerful speeches | Includes
  bibliographical references and index.
Identifiers: LCCN 2018050342 (print) | LCCN 2018057958 (ebook) |
  ISBN 9781427121844 (Electronic) |
  ISBN 9780778752400 (hardcover :alk. paper) |
  ISBN 9780778752554 (paperback :alk. paper)
Subjects: LCSH: Anthony, Susan B. (Susan Brownell),
  1820-1906--Oratory--Juvenile literature. | Anthony, Susan B.
  (Susan Brownell), 1820-1906. sears
Classification: LCC HQ1413.A55 (ebook) |
  LCC HQ1413.A55 S533 2019 (print) | DDC 305.42092--dc23
LC record available at https://lccn.loc.gov/2018050342

Crabtree Publishing Company

www.crabtreebooks.com   1-800-387-7650

Printed in the U.S.A./012019/CG20181123

**Published
in Canada
Crabtree Publishing**
616 Welland Ave.
St. Catharines, Ontario
L2M 5V6

**Published in the
United States
Crabtree Publishing**
PMB 59051
350 Fifth Avenue, 59th Floor
New York, New York 10118

**Published in the
United Kingdom
Crabtree Publishing**
Maritime House
Basin Road North, Hove
BN41 1WR

**Published
in Australia
Crabtree Publishing**
3 Charles Street
Coburg North
VIC 3058

CONTENTS

INTRODUCTION

Susan B. Anthony looked out at the crowd. More than 100 people were gathered to hear her speak. During that spring in 1873, she had addressed dozens of similar audiences across New York state. Anthony delivered the same speech each time. It was called "Is It a Crime for a U.S. Citizen to Vote?" That question was very personal to her. The 53-year-old would soon be on trial for voting **illegally**.

Anthony added the middle name "Brownell" in honor of her Aunt Susan who had that surname. Anthony backed many causes, but she is most famous for helping American women get the right to vote.

READ IT

Read the speech in full:
https://bit.ly/2QsX0f6

FIGHTING FOR RIGHTS

In the mid-1800s, American women were treated like **second-class citizens**. They had fewer rights than men did. For example, most women could not own property, have **custody** of their children, or vote. Anthony's parents raised her to believe that all people should be treated equally. Their **Quaker** faith shaped the way they lived. The family's farm became a meeting place for people who shared their views.

Anthony's father educated all seven of his children—the boys and the girls. Susan went on to become a teacher in her twenties. On the side, she fought to end slavery, and for the rights of women, workers, and students. However, she found it difficult to influence state and national leaders because she could not vote.

TIMELINE

1820   February 15, Susan Anthony born

1868   14th Amendment defined rights of American citizens

1869   NWSA founded

1870   15th Amendment gave American men of all races the right to vote

1872   November 5, Anthony voted in presidential election

1872   November 18, Anthony arrested for voting

1873   June 17–18, Anthony's trial

1906   March 13, Anthony died

1920   19th Amendment gave American women the right to vote

Susan B. Anthony's family home in Adams, Massachusetts, is now a museum. She was born there in 1820.

SUSAN B. ANTHONY
BIRTHPLACE

In 1851, Anthony met women's rights movement organizer Elizabeth Cady Stanton. They became partners with a shared goal to help improve American society. Anthony and Stanton created the National Woman Suffrage Association (NWSA) two years later. It later merged with another group to become the National American Woman Suffrage Association (NAWSA). Suffragists fought for people's right to vote in elections. Women's suffragists focused on female voters.

Anthony poured her life into the cause. She and other members of the NWSA planned to challenge voting laws in the United States. They would attempt to vote in the next presidential election. If the women were turned away, they would sue in court for their rights as citizens.

Anthony and Stanton worked together for 50 years.

VOTES FOR WOMEN A SUCCESS

Imitation Is The Sincerest Flattery!

Stanton was married and had seven children. This made it difficult for her to be away from home.

The NAWSA headquarters in 1913. The group coordinated the national suffrage movement and was predominantly run by and for educated white women.

On November 5, 1872, Anthony voted in Rochester, New York. Three of her sisters and about 11 other women joined her. They were surprised to be allowed to cast their ballots. However, they were arrested two weeks later. The male election inspectors who let them vote were arrested too.

A U.S. deputy marshal met with Anthony in the parlor of her home. He sat down with her and commented on the weather instead of getting to the point. In her words: "He hemmed and hawed and finally said Mr. Storrs [a U.S. Commissioner] wanted to see me… 'What for?' I asked. 'To arrest you,' said he. 'Is that the way you arrest men?' 'No.' Then I demanded that I should be arrested properly."

The pair took a streetcar to the police station. When the deputy marshal asked Anthony to pay her own fare, she refused. She was accused of voting "knowingly, wrongfully and unlawfully…without having a lawful right…Susan B. Anthony being then and there

Anthony voted to re-elect President Ulysses S. Grant.

Anthony's house in Rochester, New York, was where she was arrested for voting. The home is now the National Susan B. Anthony Museum & House.

a person of the female sex." U.S. Attorney Richard Crowley planned to use her case to stop other women from trying to vote too.

At the time, people charged with crimes rarely spoke in their own defense during their trials. They could speak directly to people from the community who could be called to serve on their jury, though. In the months before Anthony's trial, she toured the whole area. Her goal was to educate the people who might be her **jurors**.

Also at the time, only men could be on juries. But many women heard Anthony's speech too. She presented her case that she had the right to vote because she was an American citizen. The stakes were high. If Anthony failed to sway the public and a jury found her guilty, she faced a hefty fine or up to three years in prison. She used the newspaper coverage to increase awareness of women's suffrage across the country. This speech did more than educate New Yorkers in 1873. It summed up Anthony's whole case for women's voting rights.

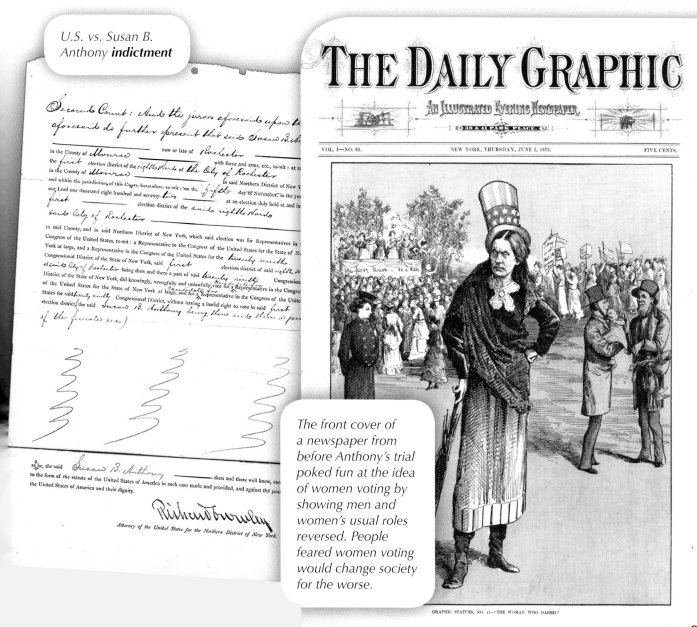

U.S. vs. Susan B. Anthony *indictment*

The front cover of a newspaper from before Anthony's trial poked fun at the idea of women voting by showing men and women's usual roles reversed. People feared women voting would change society for the worse.

PERSUASIVE PRIMARY SOURCES

Susan B. Anthony's speech is an original, firsthand account. This is called a primary source. These sources include a wide variety of text, audio, and images. Letters written by Anthony, her scrapbooks, photographs of her, and her diaries are all primary sources. Other examples include data such as voter details or election results. The **Library of Congress** in the United States calls them "raw materials." They bring us as close as we can get to being at an event or time period from history. In this case, Anthony's speech tells us about American women's voting rights in the late 1800s.

A SECOND LOOK

Secondary sources rely on information found in one or more primary sources. These materials are often made sometime after the original source was created. Another way to describe them is an interpretation. This is a kind of explanation. They usually analyze or express an opinion about someone's work or an event. Sometimes, they compare multiple points of view. The background information they provide is called context. This book is a secondary source. School textbooks are another good example.

Secondary sources, such as this book, interpret primary sources, such as this handwritten Susan B. Anthony speech. We get a clearer understanding of history by looking at both kinds of sources.

Have you ever made a video? If so, you created a primary source!

SOURCE ANALYSIS 101

Checking the following facts is the
first step in analyzing a source:

Maker, such as a writer

Intended audience

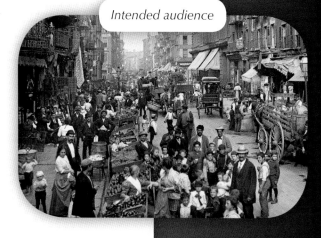

Date it was created

SPRING 1873

Purpose

Place it was delivered

Maker's point of view

COLLECTING CLUES

Details about a source are not always available in the material itself. For instance, Susan B. Anthony did not mention the date or location in her speech. This information may be found in secondary sources. Libraries, museums, and other organizations also gather all that is known about the resources in their collections. This **data** is kept in their catalogs, or databases. They can often be accessed online.

DIGGING DEEPER

Which primary source formats available today, such as audio recordings, did not exist in 1873? How could they make it easier to study the material now?

> The book stacks at the Beinecke Rare Book & Manuscript Library, Yale University, in Connecticut, house several rare books on Susan B. Anthony.

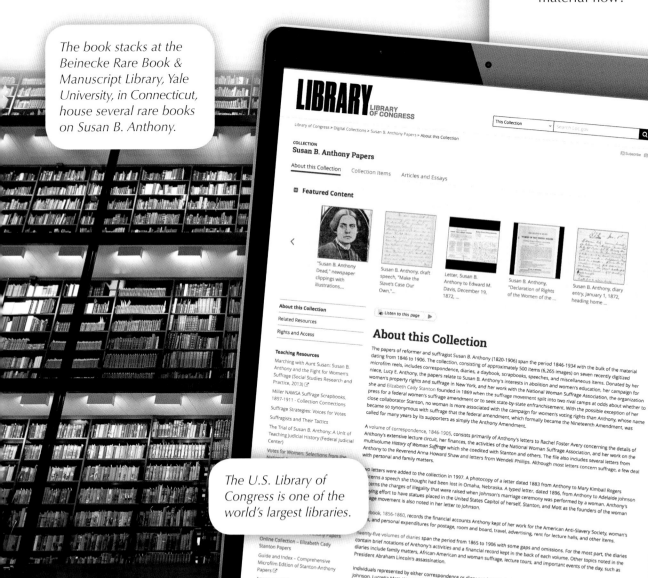

> The U.S. Library of Congress is one of the world's largest libraries.

THE FACTS

A newspaper in Rochester ran a transcript of "Is It a Crime for a U.S. Citizen to Vote?" A transcript is a printed copy of a primary source. It listed Susan B. Anthony as the maker of the speech. She started her speaking tour in Monroe County where her trial was to be held. Then the U.S. Attorney had the trial moved to Ontario County. Some people thought he did it to get a judge who would be tougher on Anthony. She simply moved her tour and kept reaching out to her jurors. In her speech, Anthony called her audience "true and **patriotic** citizens" of the United States. The purpose of the speech and her point of view are also found in the text.

Speaker:
Susan B. Anthony
Audience:
Potential jurors
at her trial
Date: 1873

> *Friends and fellow citizens…I stand before you to-night, under indictment for the alleged crime of having voted at the last Presidential election, without having a lawful right to vote. It shall be my work this evening to prove to you that in thus voting, I not only committed no crime, but, instead, simply exercised my citizen's right, guaranteed to me and all United States citizens by the National Constitution, beyond the power of any State to deny.*

The audience

Reveals that Susan B. Anthony gave this speech and hints at when she made it

The purpose of the speech

Her point of view

New York, in Anthony's case

BEHIND THE WORDS

In her speech, Anthony talked about her indictment. This is the formal charge of a crime. She was charged on January 24, 1873. Her trial was held in June. The speech that was published in the newspaper took place sometime in between those dates. Other secondary sources confirm the same speech was delivered in many places in the first half of the year. Anthony's **argument** relied on the 14th and 15th Amendments to the U.S. Constitution. The first stated that "All persons born or naturalized in the United States…are citizens…" The latter upheld that a "citizen's right to vote shall not be denied by the United States…"

PUSHING FOR CHANGE

People who push for change have a powerful tool in the spoken word. It can help boost awareness and gain support for an issue. They craft their speeches to sway audiences. Susan B. Anthony used her speech to urge people to look at women's rights in a new way. She used the following features, which are found in most persuasive speeches.

MAKING AN ARGUMENT

CLAIM

Speeches support their arguments with claims, which are statements or conclusions.

Women are paid less than men for doing the same work.

WARRANT

Warrants connect claims and evidence to support a course of action.

If women and men do the exact same work, then they should be paid the same amount.

EVIDENCE

Evidence is data or facts that prove the claims are true.

Men with full-time jobs make about 25 percent more than women who work full time.

APPEAL

Appeals in speeches urge the audience to act.

Employers must start paying men and women equally today!

INFLUENCING THE AUDIENCE

The art of persuasion used in speeches and many other texts is rhetoric. Rhetorical language uses three main ways to sway audiences.

LOGOS

Logos applies logic, or reason. It may use facts as a starting point, then draw conclusions. Logos could also begin with a general idea that is supported by facts.

All workers deserve to be treated equally. It does not make sense to pay two people different amounts if they do the same job.

ETHOS

Ethos asks the audience to side with the speaker because of his or her good character. Finding common ground, sharing personal experiences, and showing respect are all elements of ethos.

You and I both work hard to earn a living. I am sure you would agree that everyone should be paid fairly for their efforts.

PATHOS

Pathos tries to convince the audience by appealing to their emotions.

When women are paid less than men, it reveals they are still second-class citizens who do not receive fair and equal treatment.

WORDS THAT WORK

Rhetorical language is backed by devices such as:

- Using figurative language, such as **metaphors** and **similes**
- Comparing two things that are not alike in an **analogy**
- Repeating key words and phrases
- Exaggerating in **hyperboles**
- Giving things human qualities through **personification**
- Making some facts sound less important than they really are

HEARD NOT READ

When a speech is read silently instead of delivered out loud the experience is not the same. Speechwriters plan for their work to be heard. Language and voice work together to deliver the argument. Depending on the speaker, the exact same words can be presented with very different results.

Susan B. Anthony gave up to 100 speeches each year.

JOIN THE NATIONAL WOMAN SUFFRAGE ASSOCIATION

VOCAL POWER

Voice can help speakers make their points. Diction is the way someone pronounces and produces the sounds in words. It can change how the audience hears them. Diction also includes the words that are used. Switching the **tone** in which words are said can change the message. The rising and falling rhythms of those tones are called cadence. Emphasizing words or phrases is another way to stress certain points.

FORGOTTEN VOICE

There are no audio or video recordings of Susan B. Anthony. Technologies needed to record her, such as the phonograph, were not invented until later in her life. Written transcripts of her speeches are the only format available to study today. There are few details about how she sounded. There are many descriptions of male speakers from that era, however. The lack of interest in Anthony's voice may reflect society's view of women at the time.

DIGGING DEEPER

Do you think someone could make a persuasive speech without knowing anything about rhetoric? Why or why not?

CHAPTER 2

WORDS AND MEANING

To deconstruct a speech means analyzing it in a critical or detailed way. To start, read the whole source carefully. Then look for the features of the argument described in the last chapter. Watch for how rhetorical language and devices are used. Finally, gather clues that reveal how the speaker felt about the issue.

ORGANIZING IDEAS

Susan B. Anthony's speech is more than 10,000 words long. To keep the audience's interest, she presented her ideas in different ways. A comparative style uses comparison and contrast. Anthony applied it when she said women were like enslaved people, for example. Describing causes and effects is the causal way to make an argument. This is seen when Anthony defended why the 14th and 15th Amendments gave her the right to vote. Placing ideas in order is called sequential listing. This method is often used to list events. Anthony employed it when she described how she came to be charged with a crime.

PURPOSE

The reason for making a speech is its purpose. Susan B. Anthony's speech is sometimes called "On a Woman's Right to Vote." Its main argument was that she could not have committed a crime because an American citizen's right to vote was protected by the U.S. Constitution and its amendments. The purpose of the speech was to convince the men who might be on her jury that Anthony was innocent. Her greater goal was to win what she called the "battle for the **ballot**…when all United States citizens shall be recognized as equals before the law."

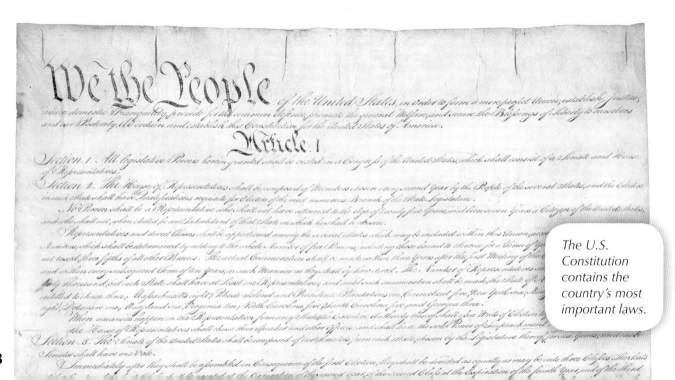

The U.S. Constitution contains the country's most important laws.

DECONSTRUCT IT

To determine the purpose of a speech, listen to it or read it and ask:
- What is the speaker's central argument?
- Who is the speaker trying to appeal to?

Speaker: *Susan B. Anthony*
Audience: *Potential jurors at her trial*
Date: *1873*

> *Are **women persons**?...I hardly believe any of our opponents will...say they are not. Being persons, then, women are citizens, and no **state** has a right to make any new law, or to enforce any old law, that shall **abridge their privileges or immunities**. Hence, every discrimination against women in the constitutions and laws of the several states, is...**null and void**... To be a person was to be a citizen, and to be a citizen was to be a voter...*

The 14th Amendment ordered that states could not "...deprive any person of... equal protection of the laws"

Anthony's fight at the time was with the state of New York

The states could not limit any rights that were made law by the U.S. Constitution

Not in force

Drawn from dictionary definitions at the time

The 14th Amendment to the Constitution addresses the rights of citizens.

CLAIMS AND EVIDENCE

Susan B. Anthony supported her argument with claims and evidence. She **cited** many facts from other sources to prove her statements. The information Anthony used was influenced by the **era**, audience, and setting. At the time, the U.S. Constitution was less than 100 years old. Three years had passed since the 15th Amendment gave African American men the right to vote. The states had been bitterly divided in the American Civil War. Now the country was rebuilding in the aftermath of that war. Questioning the powers of the government was common at the time. Examples of this are seen throughout Anthony's speech.

DECONSTRUCT IT

To find claims and evidence in a speech, ask:
- What conclusions are being made?
- Which facts or data support these statements?
- Does the speaker use their voice, such as in emphasis or pacing, to reinforce any text?

Speaker: Susan B. Anthony
Audience: Potential jurors at her trial
Date: 1873

*Our…government is based on the idea of the **natural right** of **every individual member**…to a voice and a vote in making and executing the laws…And these assertions of the **framers of the United States Constitution** of **the equal and natural rights of all the people to a voice in the government, have been affirmed and reaffirmed by the leading statesmen** of the nation, throughout the entire history of our government…*

Rights that all humans have. Elsewhere in the speech, Anthony revealed her religious background when she described it as "God-given"

Included men and women of all races in Anthony's point of view

Claims made by the men who drafted the Constitution, including George Washington and James Madison

Political leaders in the United States repeatedly upheld the importance of the rights of its citizens

Anthony's audience lived through the American Civil War.

SPEAKER SPOTLIGHT

Susan B. Anthony often wrote to people she thought might help with her causes. These letters are primary sources. She sent one to Benjamin Butler in spring 1873. Butler was a member of Congress for Massachusetts. He was known for fighting for equal rights for African Americans.

Senator Benjamin Franklin Butler helped create the Enforcement Act of 1871. It fought against racist groups such as the Ku Klux Klan.

Writer: *Susan B. Anthony*
Recipient: *Benjamin Butler*
Date: 1873

> *…all we fought for in the **late War**— the supremacy of the National Gov't to protect the rights of all persons— all citizens—against **the states' attempts to deny or abridge**…I have just **closed a canvass** of this county—from which my jurors are to be drawn—and I rather guess **the U.S. District Attorney—who is very bitter**—will hardly find twelve men so ignorant on the citizen's rights— as to agree on a verdict of Guilty…*

The civil war between the northern and southern states ended eight years earlier

The states each had different laws that could limit citizens' rights

Campaign to sway opinions on an issue

Richard Crowley was upset that Anthony was making her case in public

BEHIND THE WORDS

Anthony related women to enslaved African Americans when she referred to the "rights of all persons." The national government had recently ended slavery. Now, she wanted it to improve women's lives. Later in her letter to Butler, she described her tour of Monroe County in New York. She had done her best to persuade the men who would decide on her guilt at the trial. The letter shows her confidence that her speeches were effective.

U.S. Attorney Richard Crowley brought Susan B. Anthony to court on behalf of the Northern District of New York.

SPEAKER SPOTLIGHT

Susan B. Anthony and Elizabeth Cady Stanton started a newspaper called *The Revolution*. The NWSA published it from 1868 to 1872. It backed their goal to amend, or add to, the U.S. Constitution so that women could vote. Anthony said it was meant:

> *to educate all women to do precisely as I have done, rebel against your man-made, unjust, unconstitutional forms of law, that tax, fine, imprison and hang women, while they deny them the right of representation in the government...*

The paper used many of the same features found in speeches arguing for women's rights. The wording under the title on the front page read in part: "Men, their rights and nothing more; women, their rights and nothing less." This text summed up Anthony's view about women and men's equality.

The motto of the NWSA's newspaper was printed just under the title.

The Revolution.

PRINCIPLE, NOT POLICY: JUSTICE, NOT FAVORS.—MEN, THEIR RIGHTS AND NOTHING MORE; WOMEN, THEIR RIGHTS AND NOTHING LESS.

VOL. I.—NO. 2.   NEW YORK, WEDNESDAY, JANUARY 15, 1868. $2.00 A YEAR.

TEXAS RECONSTRUCTION.

SCARCELY a week passes in which there are not frequent murders in Texas of Union men, officers as well as others, white as well as black, and generally they go unavenged, the murderers even boasting of their bloody work! The San Antonio *Express* states that on Friday, Nov. 15, Capt. C. E. Culver, the Bureau Agent stationed at Cotton Gin, Freestone County, and his orderly, were murdered three miles north of Springfield, Limestone County. It appears that Capt. Culver had some little difficulty with one Wm. Stewart, and this same Stewart claims to have killed both Capt. Culver and his orderly, and says they fired on him first; but, strange to

path—amending the Constitution—but thus far without success. The vote in 1846 was 85,406 for, and 224,336 against impartial suffrage; in 1860 there were 197,503 in favor, and 337,984 opposed.

"The question is naturally up again in the present Convention, and may in due time come before the people; but past experience gives little hope for the friends of impartial suffrage. In the votes noted above, the Democratic party conspicuously opposed the repeal of the property qualification; a few, doubtless, voted the right way, but where one Democrat voted 'Yes,' probably ten Republicans voted 'No.'"

HOME TRUTHS.

gentleman was a man of average muscle; the four girls, as ladies go, had decidedly more than the average of physical strength.

And this is what four full-grown girls amount to! But something very like the millennium will approach before women can be made to understand that they ought to be ashamed to let one man have more strength than four women. This is the worst of it all. It is their *religious conviction* that the crowning glory of womankind is physical degeneracy. Their chief delight is to believe themselves born to cling to whatever is nearest, in a droopy, like the ivy-to-the-oak way, and to be viney, and twiney, and whiney throughout. Like the ivy to the oak, exactly, if we are willing to learn anything from

23

WARRANTS AND APPEALS

Appeals in speeches urge the audience to act. Warrants are statements that support this action. Susan B. Anthony connected her claims and evidence in warrants to convince the audience that it was not a crime for her to vote. She also appealed to wider audiences who might read her speech later. Others heard about it through secondary sources, such as opinion pieces in newspapers.

A New York Press article on Anthony's suffragist work, February 26, 1905.

DIGGING DEEPER

Why do you think lawmakers did not view American women as full citizens in 1873? What reasons might they have had for resisting women's suffrage?

DECONSTRUCT IT

Find warrants and appeals in a speech by asking:
- Is the speaker urging the audience to act or think a certain way?
- How are claims and evidence being connected to convince them?

Speaker: Susan B. Anthony
Audience: Potential jurors at her trial
Date: 1873

PART THREE

ESIDENT,

y's Home

writing an address to be delivered at another congress in Oregon next summer. Incidentally she will deliver a few impromptu addresses elsewhere. Her correspondence with local branches of the National Association of Woman Suffragists the length and breadth of the land is voluminous. She is very punctilious about answering letters. Until she was past 80 she used to write them all in longhand. Now she uses a typewriter, with the result, she says, that her letters are about twice as long as they should be.

Miss Anthony's dress is simplicity itself, the quiet, simple gray gown of the Quaker. Her fingers are unencumbered by rings. The only thing she wears in the way of jewelry is a small watch chain. Her hair is by no means white. It is iron-gray, indi-

> ...We no longer **petition Legislature or Congress** to give us the right to vote. We appeal to women everywhere to exercise their too long neglected "citizen's right to vote." We appeal to the **inspectors of election** everywhere to receive the votes of all United States citizens as it is their duty to do. We appeal to United States **commissioners and marshals** to arrest the inspectors who reject the names and votes of United States citizens...and leave those alone who, like our **eighth ward inspectors**, perform their duties faithfully and well. **We ask the juries to fail to return verdicts of "guilty" against honest, law-abiding, tax-paying United States citizens for offering their votes at our elections...**

Make requests to these two levels of the United States government

Staff working at voting polls

The same people who arrested Anthony

Who allowed the women to vote in Rochester in November 1872

This is a direct appeal to potential jurors at Anthony's trial

SPEAKER SPOTLIGHT

The word "petition" can mean an action or a written request. The written kind of petition is a primary source. This form is usually signed by many people. It shows who supported a certain point of view at the time. In January 1866, Susan B. Anthony and other women's suffragists appealed to the United States Congress which was about to extend voting rights to African American men. "A Petition for Universal Suffrage" urged them to update the Constitution so women could vote legally.

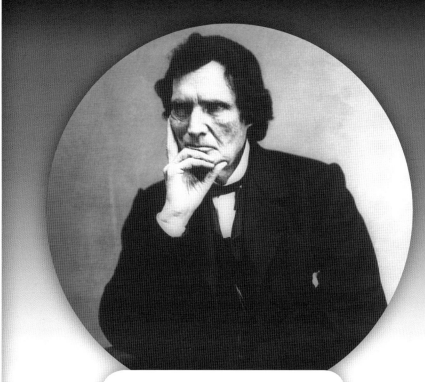

Congressman Thaddeus Stevens gave the petition to the government on Anthony and Stanton's behalf in 1866.

Writers: U.S. women suffragists
Audience: U.S. Congress
Date: 1866

" *The **undersigned, Women of the United States**, respectfully ask an amendment of the Constitution that shall prohibit the several States from **disfranchising** any of their citizens **on the ground of sex**…as you are now amending the Constitution, and, in harmony with **advancing civilization**, placing new safeguards round the individual rights of four millions of emancipated slaves, we ask that you extend the right of Suffrage to Woman—the only remaining class of disfranchised citizens…* "

People who signed the petition
The text highlighted that they represented half of country
Denying the right to vote
Because they are women
They made changes after the American Civil War
Refers to changing points of view regarding African Americans

A PETITION

FOR

UNIVERSAL SUFFRAGE.

To the Senate and House of Representatives:

The undersigned, Women of the United States, respectfully ask an amendment of the Constitution that shall prohibit the several States from disfranchising any of their citizens on the ground of sex.

In making our demand for Suffrage, we would call your attention to the fact that we represent fifteen million people—one half the entire population of the country—intelligent, virtuous, native-born American citizens; and yet stand outside the pale of political recognition.

The Constitution classes us as "free people," and counts us *whole* persons in the basis of representation; and yet are we governed without our consent, compelled to pay taxes without appeal, and punished for violations of law without choice of judge or juror.

The experience of all ages, the Declarations of the Fathers, the Statute Laws of our own day, and the fearful revolution through which we have just passed, all prove the uncertain tenure of life, liberty and property so long as the ballot—the only weapon of self-protection—is not in the hand of every citizen.

Therefore, as you are now amending the Constitution, and, in harmony with advancing civilization, placing new safeguards round the individual rights of four millions of emancipated slaves, we ask that you extend the right of Suffrage to Woman—the only remaining class of disfranchised citizens—and thus fulfil your Constitutional obligation "to Guarantee to every State in the Union a Republican form of Government."

As all partial application of Republican principles must ever breed a complicated legislation as well as a discontented people, we would pray your Honorable Body, in order to simplify the machinery of government and ensure domestic tranquillity, that you legislate hereafter for persons, citizens, tax-payers, and not for class or caste.

For justice and equality your petitioners will ever pray.

NAMES.	RESIDENCE.
Emily Stanton,	New York
Susan B. Anthony	Rochester – N.Y.
Antoinette Brown Blackwell	New York
Lucy Stone	Newark N. Jersey
Joanna S. Morse	
Ernestine L. Rose	48 Livingston. Brooklyn New York
Harriet E. Eaton	6, West 14th Street N.Y.
Catharine C. Wilkeson	83 Clinton Place
Elizabeth R. Tilton	
Mary Fowler Gilbert	48 Livingston
Mary S. Gilbert	295 W. 19th St N.
M. Griffith	New York

The first two signatures on this petition belong to Elizabeth Cady Stanton and Susan B. Anthony.

27

RHETORICAL LANGUAGE

Rhetorical language helps speakers present claims and support them with evidence, and make appeals and warrants. Susan B. Anthony used logos as she quoted other sources widely during her speech. These included speeches made by **notable** American leaders and lawmakers, such as James Madison, the U.S. Supreme Court, and Benjamin Franklin. In addition, she called on important documents such as the Articles of Confederation from 1781 and the U.S. Constitution. Anthony also used pathos as a persuasive strategy, as is seen in the first excerpt below. The second section shows ethos, as she presented herself.

DECONSTRUCT IT

To identify the rhetorical language in a speech, ask:
- How is the speaker using logic and reason to persuade the audience?
- Does the speaker's character help support the central argument?
- How is the audience being swayed by emotion?

Speaker: Susan B. Anthony
Audience: Potential jurors at her trial
Date: 1873

> ...*The women, **dissatisfied as they are with this form of government**, that enforces taxation without representation— that **compels** them to obey laws to which they have never given their **consent**, that imprisons and hangs them without a trial by a jury of their **peers**, that **robs them, in marriage, of the custody of their own persons, wages and children**—are this half of the people left wholly at the mercy of the other half, in direct violation of the spirit and letter of the declarations of the framers of this government, every one of which was based on the immutable principle of equal rights to all?*

Quote phrase	Explanation
	Which treated them unfairly because they were not men
	Compared American women to colonists in the 1700s, who *railed* against paying taxes to Britain without having any elected leaders to speak for them
	Women could not be jurors
	A husband had legal authority over his wife, her possessions, and even their children
	The intended meaning and actual wording of the Declaration of Independence, the U.S. Constitution, and other important documents that highlighted equality
	A rule that cannot be challenged

28

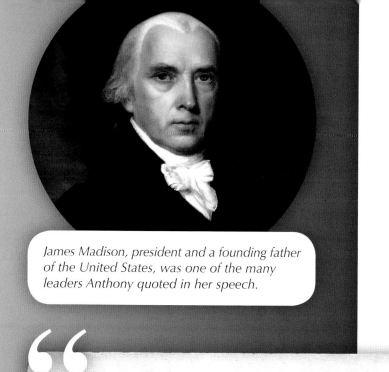

James Madison, president and a founding father of the United States, was one of the many leaders Anthony quoted in her speech.

BEHIND THE WORDS

Anthony intended to stir up sympathy in her audience with these claims. Speaking about robbing women of their rights is an example of pathos. It plays on people's emotions. Anthony stressed that with no ability to vote, women had no influence over the laws they still had to keep. She also used rhetorical devices such as run-on sentences. They built up **momentum** and overflowed with passion.

Speaker: Susan B. Anthony
Audience: Potential jurors at her trial
Date: 1873

*...But, **friends**, when in accordance with Senator Sumner's counsel, I went to the ballot-box last November, and exercised my citizen's right to vote, the courts **did not wait for me to appeal to them— they appealed to me**, and indicted me on the charge of having voted illegally...*

Ethos finds common ground with the audience

Gained credibility by showing she was powerful enough to consult with a U.S. senator and that he agreed with her stand

She stated this as fact

Play on words

Men are lined up to vote at a polling booth.

DIGGING DEEPER

Susan B. Anthony and her opponents both believed that the 14th Amendment supported their own arguments. How does someone's point of view influence how they present facts?

29

CHAPTER 3

ANALYZING PERSPECTIVES

Speeches often reveal how the maker felt about an issue at a certain time in history. The person who gives a speech is not always the one who writes it, though. The writer tries to use the speaker's perspective, or point of view. Susan B. Anthony and Elizabeth Cady Stanton were known to work together on speeches. Stanton was the "ideas person" in the duo. Anthony was skilled at persuasively presenting their shared point of view.

CHANGING TIMES

The era when a speech is made also affects perspective. Both the maker and the audience are products of their time. Today, Anthony would not ask if it was a crime for a woman to vote. American society's point of view on the issue has changed since the 19th century. In 1873, many people accepted the fact that women did not have the same rights as men did. It was simply how their world worked.

American white **suffragettes** pose before a street march in 1911. Over the years, the NAWSA became more **exclusionary** in race and **class**. African American women formed their own suffrage organizations such as the Alpha Suffrage Club.

DIGGING DEEPER

Do you think everyone is treated equally in society today? Why or why not?

INFLUENCING PERSPECTIVE

Nuanced language uses words to create a feeling that sways the audience. These word choices can also show the speechmaker's perspective. For example, Anthony talked about "God-given rights" in the U.S. Constitution and the Declaration of Independence. This highlighted her own religious roots, as well as the country's. The language implies that an ultimate authority is on her side. Later, Anthony used "legal right" to describe laws imposed by the state. This makes a **distinction** between rights given by God and rights given by people. This is just one of the ways Anthony used rhetoric to persuade her audience.

DECONSTRUCT IT

To examine a speaker's perspective, ask:
- How does the language used show the speaker's feelings?
- How could the speaker's point of view be summed up in one sentence?

> **Speaker:** *Susan B. Anthony*
> **Audience:** *Potential jurors at her trial*
> **Date:** *1873*

> *It was **we, the people**, not we, the white male citizens, nor yet we, the male citizens; but **we, the whole people, who formed this Union**… And it is **downright mockery** to talk to women of their enjoyment of the **blessings of liberty** while they are denied the use of the only means of securing them…**the ballot**…To them this government is not a **democracy**… It is an **odious aristocracy**…which makes father, brothers, husband, sons, the **oligarchs** over the mother and sisters, the wife and daughters of every household; which ordains all men **sovereigns**, all women **subjects**, carries **dissension**, **discord** and **rebellion** into every home of the nation…*

Quoted the beginning of the U.S. Constitution
This became one of Anthony's most famous quotations
Loaded language is found throughout the speech
The good things that come from having freedom
Voting allowed citizens to choose who would make decisions on their behalf

BEHIND THE WORDS

Anthony's audience believed they lived in a system in which everyone's voice was heard. However, more than half of the country's population could not vote. Anthony argued that men ruled like kings with complete control. Women were their subjects who could only do what the rulers allowed. She felt this imbalance led to conflicts between women and men.

HITTING THE LIMIT

Primary sources such as speeches usually have a single point of view. Susan B. Anthony only shared the evidence that helped her case. For example, she did not talk about the court verdicts that had ruled against women's rights in the United States. She made no mention of the women who rallied against their own suffrage. Anthony did not point out that some women's suffragists did not believe in equal rights for African American women. Her speech left out all these facts. This shows why it is important to look beyond the single perspective of one maker.

DECONSTRUCT IT

To find the limitations of a speech, ask:
- How does the maker's perspective shape this primary source?
- Are any important details being left out?
- Based on evidence from other sources, are there any points that should be explored further?

Speaker: *Susan B. Anthony*
Audience: *Potential jurors at her trial*
Date: *1873*

> *I stand before you to-night, under indictment for the **alleged crime** of having voted at the last Presidential election, without having a lawful right to vote…We all know that American citizenship, without addition or qualification, means the possession of equal rights, civil and political…There is an old saying that "a rose by any other name would smell as sweet," and I submit it the deprivation by law of the ownership of one's own person, wages, property, children, the denial of the right as an individual, to sue and be sued, and to testify in the courts, is not a condition of servitude most bitter and absolute, though under the sacred name of marriage?…*

Anthony disagreed with it, but she had committed a crime according to the laws of her day

But not everyone agreed

Women were not the only group who did not possess these rights

Quoted William Shakespeare's play *Romeo and Juliet*

Described the legal denial of these rights to women that most American men held in 1873

BEHIND THE WORDS

In her speech, Anthony compared married women to enslaved people. She argued that both were denied rights and freedoms. This is her personal perspective as a white woman. Anthony did not reflect on how an African American might view this claim.

OTHER PERSPECTIVES

The makers of speeches are not the only ones with a perspective. The way they address the audience may reveal the crowd's point of view. Susan B. Anthony's speech appealed to educated and open-minded Americans, for example. The creators of secondary sources also have their own perspectives and **biases**. This can lead to different conclusions being made about the same speech. Looking at multiple sources gives the best insight. Review materials from the same time period to find out how other people felt about the issue.

This Harper's Weekly *cover from 1907 shows anti-suffragist women appealing to lawmakers to "save women" from themselves.*

Writer and activist Ida B. Wells fought for women's rights. Not treated as an equal by white suffragists, she helped form her own suffrage association for African American women, the Alpha Suffrage Club.

Louis Brandeis was a Supreme Court justice who by 1915 was giving speeches in support of women's suffrage.

33

"AIN'T I A WOMAN?"

Sojourner Truth was born into slavery in the late 1790s. She gained her freedom in 1826. Truth became a preacher who fought to end slavery. Like Susan B. Anthony, she was a suffragist. However, the two women came from very different backgrounds. Anthony was a teacher, whereas Truth did not have the opportunity to learn to read or write. Their experiences shaped their perspectives and their speeches. One of Truth's most famous addresses was made at a convention for women's rights in 1851. Unlike the facts from government sources that Anthony used, Truth relied on everyday activities as evidence. She spoke without any notes. The closest version of this speech was written down by Marius Robinson. He was in the audience the day she gave it. Later, he printed what he remembered of it in *The Anti-Slavery Bugle* newspaper.

Women's Rights Convention.
Sojourner Truth.

One of the most unique and interesting speeches of the Convention was made by Sojourner Truth, an emancipated slave. It is impossible to transfer it to paper, or convey any adequate idea of the effect it produced upon the audience. Those only can appreciate it who saw her powerful form, her whole-souled, earnest gesture, and listened to her strong and truthful tones. She came forward to the platform and addressing the President said with great simplicity:

May I say a few words? Receiving an affirmative answer, she proceeded; I want to say a few words about this matter. I am a woman's rights. I have as much muscle as any man, and can do as much work as any man. I have plowed and reaped and husked and chopped and mowed, and can any man do more than that? I have heard much about the sexes being equal; I can carry as much as any man, and can eat as much too, if I can get it. I am as strong as any man that is now. As for intellect, all I can say is, if woman have a pint and man a quart—why cant she have her little pint full? You need not be afraid to give us our rights for fear we will take too much,—for we cant take more than our pint'll hold. The poor men seem to be all in confusion, and dont know what to do. Why children, if you have woman's rights give it to her and you will feel better. You will have your own rights, and they wont be so much trouble. I cant read, but I can hear. I have heard the bible and have learned that Eve caused man to sin. Well if woman upset the world, do give her a chance to set it right side up again. The Lady has spoken about Jesus, how he never spurned woman from him, and she was right. When Lazarus died, Mary and Martha came to him with faith and love and besought him to raise their brother. And Jesus wept—and Lazarus came forth. And how came Jesus into the world? Through God who created him and woman who bore him. Man, where is your part? But the women are coming up blessed be God and a few of the men are coming up with them. But man is in a tight place, the poor slave is on him, woman is coming on him, and he is surely between a hawk and a buzzard.

> ...*I have as much muscle as any man and can do as much work as any man. I have plowed and reaped and husked and chopped and mowed, and can any man do more than that? I have heard much about the sexes being equal...As for intellect, all I can say is, if a woman have a pint, and a man a quart—why can't she have her little pint full?...The poor men seems to be all in confusion, and don't know what to do. Why children, if you have woman's rights, give it to her and you will feel better. You will have your own rights, and they won't be so much trouble...But man is in a tight place, the poor slave is on him, woman is coming on him, he is surely between a hawk and a buzzard.*

Speaker:
Sojourner Truth
Audience:
Women's Rights Convention in Akron, Ohio
Date: 1851

Pointed out that there were women who had double the powers of reason and understanding that some men had

Language showed lack of sympathy for these poor, confused men

A simple appeal compared to Anthony's speech

Argued that giving women equal rights would not take away men's rights

Speech was given in the lead-up to the civil war, which prompted the end of slavery in the United States

Phrase used at the time meant being stuck between two dangerous groups

BEHIND THE WORDS

Equality was one of the goals of the founders of the United States. Most of 19th-century American society saw a natural inequality between men and women, however. Sojourner Truth believed that women were both physically and mentally equal to men. She saw evidence of it in her own life. From Truth's perspective, this equality should have been extended to voting rights for all.

WATCH IT

View videos of women reading Sojourner Truth's speech at **www.thesojournertruthproject. com/the-readings**

Sojourner Truth worked for universal suffrage, which called for voting rights for everyone.

Suffragist Frances Dana Barker Gage rewrote Truth's speech in 1863. This version is still popular today but it is not true to the primary source.

Marius Robinson was a minister and a friend of Sojourner Truth.

OPPOSING SUFFRAGE

The National Association Opposed to Woman Suffrage (NAOWS) formed in the United States in the early 1900s. The group fought against women getting the right to vote. The NAOWS was mostly women, including its prominent president, Josephine Jewell Dodge. In 1919, it had around 500,000 members. They published a newsletter called *The Woman's Protest Against Woman Suffrage*. The group also gave out pamphlets to educate Americans on the dangers of women voting.

Writers: NAOWS members
Audience: NAOWS newsletter readers
Date: Unknown

Vote NO on Woman Suffrage

BECAUSE 90% of the women **do not want it**, *or* **do not care**.

BECAUSE it means **competition of women with men instead of co-operation**.

BECAUSE **80% of the women eligible to vote are married** *and* **can only double or annul their husbands' votes**.

BECAUSE **it can be of no benefit commensurate with the additional expense involved**.

BECAUSE in some States more voting women than voting men will place the Government under **petticoat rule**.

BECAUSE it is unwise to **risk the good we already have for the evil which may occur**.

Annotations
Used data as evidence but did not cite source
Point of view of the NAOWS
Equated some women's willingness to be treated as lesser than men with them working together
Cited more facts without a source
Suggested that if a husband and wife voted for the same person, it was an unfair advantage, and if they voted for different people, they would cancel out each other
Basically, it would be so expensive to put into place, it was not worth doing
Referred to a government overly influenced by women
Played on people's fears of the unknown

Vote NO on Woman Suffrage

BECAUSE 90% of the women either do not want it, or *do not care.*

BECAUSE it means *competition* of women with men instead of *co-operation.*

BECAUSE 80% of the women eligible to vote are married and can only double or annul their husbands' votes.

BECAUSE it can be of no benefit commensurate with the additional expense involved.

BECAUSE in some States more voting women than voting men will place the Government under petticoat rule.

BECAUSE it is unwise to risk the good we already have for the evil which may occur.

BEHIND THE WORDS

The facts presented by the NAOWS were the point of view of the group's members. They feared petticoat rule, which was a **scornful** way of suggesting a government overly influenced by women. The pamphlet played on fears of the unknown. It offered "facts" but did not cite any sources. It suggested that a woman's willingness to be treated as inferior, or lower than a man, was the same as them working together. It also concluded that the "one person, one vote" idea put forward by those who preached equality, should not apply to married women. They also argued that giving women the vote was not worth doing because it would be expensive and would not change things.

DIGGING DEEPER

People who were against women's suffrage often came from well-off backgrounds. They already had power and freedom. How might this have influenced their perspectives?

The front window of the NAOWS headquarters displayed reasons why women should not vote.

Women who were anti-suffragists tended to come from wealthy, powerful families.

CHAPTER 4

INFLUENCES THEN AND NOW

Did Susan B. Anthony's speech win over her jurors? It is impossible to know. Judge Ward Hunt ordered the jury to find Anthony guilty. They never got the chance to discuss their views. This was very unusual. Later, the judge was accused of being hostile to the cause of women's suffrage.

NO NEW TRIAL

Judge Ward fined Anthony $100 as punishment. In today's dollars, that works out to more than $2,000. She refused to pay the fine. That would usually land someone in prison, which was actually Anthony's goal. People who were imprisoned could get a new trial. For this reason, the court did not go after Anthony for not paying her fine. This blocked her from taking her case any further.

Susan B. Anthony devoted her life to women's suffrage, as well as other causes she felt strongly about.

Judge Ward Hunt

SPEAKER SPOTLIGHT

After Anthony was found guilty, the judge asked if she had any reason why he should not announce his sentence. This was a standard question. No one recorded her reply that day in June 1873. However, there were a few later accounts. Anthony herself wrote *An Account of the Proceedings on the Trial of Susan B. Anthony* the next year.

DIGGING DEEPER

Susan B. Anthony's account of what she said to the judge is much longer than the other two known versions. What are some possible problems with recalling what someone said later on?

" *Yes, your honor, I have many things to say...I am degraded from the status of a citizen to that of a subject; and not only myself individually, but all of my sex, are, by your honor's verdict, doomed to* **political subjection** *under this, so-called, form of government...the same man-made forms of law, declared it a crime punishable with $1,000 fine and six months' imprisonment...to give a cup of cold water, a crust of bread, or a night's shelter to a* **panting fugitive as he was tracking his way to Canada.** *And every man or woman in whose veins coursed a drop of human sympathy* **violated that wicked law, reckless of consequences, and was justified in so doing**...*When I was brought before your honor for trial,* **I hoped for a broad and liberal interpretation of the Constitution and its recent amendments,** *that should declare...equality of rights the national guarantee to all persons born or naturalized in the United States...* "

Being under the control of the group in power

Referred to an enslaved person following the trail to freedom outside of the country

Basically anyone with feelings

Excused her crime by comparing it to breaking another unjust law

Described her overall goal

Speaker: Susan B. Anthony
Audience: American public
Date: 1874

Women's suffragists made Anthony's "Failure is impossible" quotation into a slogan.

FAILURE IS IMPOSSIBLE!

After the trial, women's suffragists kept meeting at Anthony's home in Rochester. It became the headquarters for the National American Woman Suffrage Association. The group continued to petition the government to amend the U.S. Constitution so women could vote. Anthony even met with President Theodore Roosevelt on behalf of the NAWSA in 1905. She gave her last speech at a party for her 86th birthday. During this address, she famously declared, "Failure is impossible!" Anthony died a month after her birthday in 1906.

SIGNIFICANT SPEECH

Susan B. Anthony battled for women's suffrage for decades. However, she did not live to see women get the vote. Her "Is It a Crime for a U.S. Citizen to Vote?" speech was one of hundreds that she gave over the years. She inspired many other suffragists to carry on with the fight. They finally succeeded in 1920. The 19th Amendment to the U.S. Constitution gave American women over the age of 21 the right to vote. It is known informally as the "Anthony Amendment" because of her efforts.

International Film Service
SPEAKER GILLETT SIGNING THE SUFFRAGE BILL
The bill providing for a Constitutional Amendment granting the suffrage to women throughout the Nation was signed, as shown above, by the Speaker of the House of Representatives after it had been passed by the Senate

H. J. Res. 1.   5

Sixty-sixth Congress of the United States of America;

At the First Session,

Begun and held at the City of Washington on Monday, the nineteenth day of May, one thousand nine hundred and nineteen.

JOINT RESOLUTION

Proposing an amendment to the Constitution extending the right of suffrage to women.

Resolved by the Senate and House of Representatives of the United States of America in Congress assembled (two-thirds of each House concurring therein), That the following article is proposed as an amendment to the Constitution, which shall be valid to all intents and purposes as part of the Constitution when ratified by the legislatures of three-fourths of the several States.

"ARTICLE —

"The right of citizens of the United States to vote shall not be denied or abridged by the United States or by any State on account of sex.

"Congress shall have power to enforce this article by appropriate legislation."

F. H. Gillett
Speaker of the House of Representatives.

Thos. R. Marshall
Vice President of the United States and
President of the Senate.

19th Amendment

41

CHANGING PERSPECTIVES

Over time, people's attitudes slowly changed. It became clear that women were treated unfairly. American society today shares the belief in equality. Women have gained many rights they lacked in 1873. They are now represented in government. However, if Anthony were alive now, she would see areas where inequality still exists. New voices are expanding the idea of true equality and arguing for equal rights for all.

TODAY'S VOICES

In the 1800s, suffragists used methods such as speeches, petitions, and pamphlets to tell people about their cause. Today, activists have a much wider audience thanks to the Internet. New media, such as social networks and online videos, spread the word around the world almost instantly. The delivery method has changed, but words are still powerful and are used as vehicles for change.

Some modern American voters place the stickers they get at voting booths on Susan B. Anthony's tombstone.

GET OUT AND VOTE

Public figures often use their fame to appeal to audiences. Before the American presidential election in 2016, singer Beyoncé delivered a speech. It was at a concert encouraging people to vote. Her argument revealed how far the United States has come from being a country in which suffragists struggled for the right to vote. Now it is one in which people must be urged to fight apathy, or indifference. They must be encouraged to get out and cast their ballots.

Speaker: *Beyoncé*
Audience: *Fans attending a Jay Z concert to inspire voters in Cleveland, Ohio*
Date: *Nov. 4, 2016*

> *There was a time when a woman's opinion did not matter. If you were **black**, **white**, **Mexican**, **Asian**, **Muslim**, educated, poor or rich; if you were a woman, it did not matter. Less than 100 years ago, women did not have the right to vote. **Look how far we've come from having no voice to being on the brink of making history—again—by electing the first woman president.** Yes! But we **have** to vote. **The world looks to us as a progressive country that leads change**…I want my daughter to grow up seeing a woman lead our country and know that her possibilities are limitless.*

These are among the many groups that Anthony overlooked in her speech

In 2008, the United States elected its first African American president, Barack Obama

Beyoncé campaigned for Hillary Clinton

Emphasized this word to show the importance of voting

Used pathos as a persuasive strategy on her American audience

Compares how far American society has come to when Anthony fought for her rights as a citizen

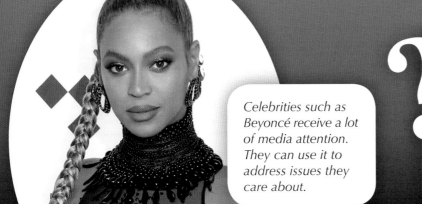

Celebrities such as Beyoncé receive a lot of media attention. They can use it to address issues they care about.

DIGGING DEEPER

Just over half of Americans who could vote did so in the 2016 presidential election. Why do you think so many people did not bother to vote? How would you convince someone that it is important to vote?

BIBLIOGRAPHY

INTRODUCTION

"About the Susan B. Anthony Museum & House." National Susan B. Anthony Museum & House. susanbanthonyhouse.org/blog

"Collection: Susan B. Anthony Papers." Library of Congress. https://bit.ly/2QLxyAQ

"Freedom Exhibition." U.S. Capitol Visitor Center. https://bit.ly/2QICJS0

Glass, Andrew. "Susan B. Anthony found guilty of voting, June 19, 1873." *Politico*, June 19, 2018. https://politi.co/2PBdzEw

Gordon, Ann D. *The Selected Papers of Elizabeth Cady Stanton and Susan B. Anthony: Against an Aristocracy of Sex, 1866 to 1873*. New Jersey: Rutgers University Press, 2000.

Gordon, Ann D. *The Trial of Susan B. Anthony*. Washington: Federal Judicial History Office, Federal Judicial Center, 2005.

Harper, Ida Husted. "Susan B. Anthony: The Woman and Her Work." *The North American Review*, *182*(593), Vol. 182 No. 593 (April 1906): 604–616.

"Lesson Module: Women's Suffrage in the United States." Eagleton Institute of Politics, Rutgers University. https://bit.ly/2RGv0Fj

Linder, Doug. "The Trial of Susan B. Anthony for Illegal Voting." Famous Trials, 2001. https://bit.ly/2C8Ty4w

Onion, Rebecca. "Susan B. Anthony's Indictment for Voting While Female." *Slate*, March 6, 2014. https://bit.ly/1hPShhj

Peck, Ira. "Susan B. Anthony Dares to Vote!" *Junior Scholastic*, March 10, 1989. https://bit.ly/2A5Rb14

"Susan B. Anthony voted on this date in 1872, leading to her arrest." Read Write Think. https://bit.ly/2ybRCFC

"Timeline." The Elizabeth Cady Stanton & Susan B. Anthony Papers Project. http://ecssba. rutgers.edu/resources/timeline.html

"United States v. Anthony: Federal Trials and Great Debates in United States History." Federal Judicial Center. https://bit.ly/2QLJd2B

"Women's Rights." U.S. History. www.ushistory. org/us/26c.asp

CHAPTER 1

Fahnestock, Jeanne. *Rhetorical Style: The Uses of Language in Persuasion*. New York: Oxford University Press, 2011.

McIntyre, Catherine. "Why do men make more money than women?" *Maclean's*, February 8, 2018. https://bit.ly/2ydId02

"Primary Sources." University of California Irvine Libraries. www.lib.uci.edu/introduction-primary-sources

"Primary Sources: What Are They?" Teaching History. teachinghistory.org/best-practices/using-primary-sources/19079

"Primary vs. Secondary Sources." BMCC Library. lib1.bmcc.cuny.edu/help/sources

"Susan B. Anthony: On Women's Right to Vote." Great American Documents. https://bit.ly/2QsX0f6

"Susan B. Anthony: On Women's Right to Vote." The History Place: Great Speeches Collection. www.historyplace.com/speeches/anthony.htm

"Using Primary Sources." United States Library of Congress. www.loc.gov/teachers/usingprimarysources

Weida, Stacy, and Karl Stolley. "Using Rhetorical Strategies for Persuasion." Purdue Online Writing Lab. https://owl.purdue.edu/owl/general_writing/academic_writing/establishing_arguments/rhetorical_strategies.html

CHAPTER 2

Anthony, Susan B. *An account of the proceedings on the trial of Susan B. Anthony*. Rochester: Daily Democrat and Chronicle Book Print, 1874.

"Benjamin F. Butler." *Encyclopedia Britannica*, November 1, 2018. https://bit.ly/2CEtYp8

"Petition for Universal Suffrage 1866." The Elizabeth Cady Stanton & Susan B. Anthony Papers Project. http://ecssba.rutgers.edu/docs/petuniv.html

"Remarks by Susan B. Anthony in the Circuit Court of the United States for the Northern District of New York, 19 June 1873." The Elizabeth Cady Stanton & Susan B. Anthony Papers Project. http://ecssba.rutgers.edu/docs/sbatrial.html

"Suffragists Organize: National Woman Suffrage Association." National Women's History Museum. www.crusadeforthevote.org/nwsa-organize

"The Revolution." Accessible Archives. https://bit.ly/2Pvc1vW

CHAPTER 3

"American Women Who Were Anti-Suffragettes." NPR History Department, October 22, 2015. https://n.pr/2Oo6BX1

Barkhorn, Eleanor. "'Vote No on Women's Suffrage': Bizarre Reasons For Not Letting Women Vote." *The Atlantic*, November 6, 2012. https://bit.ly/2MZU9eR

"Guide to the Josephine Jewell Dodge Papers, 1873–1874." Vassar College Libraries. https://bit.ly/2NBX75e

"Marius R. Robinson (1806–1878)." The African-American Experience in Ohio, 1850–1920. https://bit.ly/2NNtZJd

Massie, Victoria. "3 black women who fought on the front lines for women's suffrage." *Complex*, October 15, 2015. https://bit.ly/2EfgiCq

Miller, Joe C. "Never A Fight of Woman Against Man: What Textbooks Don't Say about Women's Suffrage." *The History Teacher, 48*(3), (May 2015): 438–482. https://bit.ly/2pQjBpP

"National Association Opposed to Woman Suffrage." National Women's History Museum. www.crusadeforthevote.org/naows-opposition

"Pamphlet distributed by the National Association Opposed to Woman Suffrage." Jewish Women's Archive. https://bit.ly/2oxZNXE

"People & Ideas: Susan B. Anthony." God in America, *PBS*. https://to.pbs.org/2hzsO1K

"Sojourner Truth." Sojourner Truth Memorial Committee. https://sojournertruthmemorial.org

"Stanton/Anthony Friendship." Susan B. Anthony Center, University of Rochester. https://bit.ly/2yvWowT

"Why is there more than one version of Sojourner Truth's famous 1851, 'Ain't I a Woman' speech?" The Sojourner Truth Project. www.thesojournertruthproject.com

CHAPTER 4

Beyoncé. Instagram, November 5, 2016. https://bit.ly/2PBqsOR

DeSilver, Drew. "U.S. trails most developed countries in voter turnout." Pew Research Center, May 21, 2018. https://pewrsr.ch/2GEUyvO

Kreps, Daniel. "See Beyoncé's Powerful Speech at Jay Z's Hillary Clinton Rally." *Rolling Stone*, November 5, 2016. https://bit.ly/2A5ttSp

LEARNING MORE

BOOKS

Colman, Penny. *Elizabeth Cady Stanton and Susan B. Anthony: A Friendship That Changed the World*. New York: Square Fish, 2016.

Conkling, Winifred. *Votes for Women! American Suffragists and the Battle for the Ballot*. Chapel Hill: Algonquin Young Readers, 2018.

Kendall, Martha E. *Susan B. Anthony: Fighter for Women's Voting Rights*. New York: Enslow Publishing, 2015.

WEBSITES

Learn more about the other causes that Susan B. Anthony fought for: **https://bit.ly/2pPGny8**

Get more information about women fighting for the right to vote: **https://bit.ly/2yBE5q6**

Follow the women's suffrage timeline to see the progress since 1776: **https://bit.ly/2oZkJIO**

GLOSSARY

analogy A similarity between two things from which a comparison is made

argument A discussion or debate involving different points of view

aristocracy A class of people considered elite and who hold rank and privilege, or unearned benefits beyond what others have

ballot A piece of paper on which a voter marks their vote

biases Opinions in favor of or against a person, group, or thing, usually in an unfair way

cited Quoted or mentioned as an example or evidence in support, proof, or confirmation of a fact

class A system of dividing people based on their social and or economic privilege or lack of privilege

compels Forces or pressures someone to do something

consent Permission for something to happen or agreement to do something

custody Guardianship or care of someone

data Facts, statistics, or information

democracy A system in which people vote to elect people to represent them in government

discord A state or condition marked by a lack of agreement

dissension Disagreement that leads to conflict and discord

distinction A difference or contrast between similar things

era A period of time marked by specific events

exclusionary Shutting out a person or group and preventing them from participating

hyperbole Obvious and intentional exaggeration

illegally In a way that is forbidden by law

indictment A formal charge or accusation of a serious crime

jurors A group of people sworn to deliver a verdict, or judgment, in a court case

Library of Congress The research library of the United States Congress that also serves as a national library

metaphors Figures of speech in which a term or phrase is used to represent something else

momentum The force or strength that allows something to continue or to grow stronger or faster as time passes, or that keeps an event developing after it has started

notable Worthy of attention or notice

odious Something considered disgusting, offensive, or hateful

oligarchs The rulers in a form of government in which power is held by one class or group

patriotic Having and showing great love and support for one's country

peers People of the same age, status, or abilities as another specific person

personification Giving human qualities to an animal, object, or idea

Quaker A member of a religious group called the Religious Society of Friends, whose beliefs included equality and social reform

railed Complained or strongly protested

rebellion Resisting authority, control, or the way things are usually done

scornful Full of scorn, contempt, or dislike

second-class citizens People who are denied full social, political, and economic benefits of citizenship, despite their status as citizens of a country

similes Figures of speech in which two things that are not alike are compared

sovereigns Kings or queens or other supreme rulers

subjects People who are under the rule of a sovereign, or people who have sworn allegiance to a government and live under its protection

suffragettes Women who advocated, or worked in favor of, female voting rights

INDEX

ABOUT THE AUTHOR

Rebecca Sjonger is the author of more than 50 nonfiction books for young people. American history is one of her favorite subjects to write about. She loves the challenge of separating facts from fiction while researching.